ALL ABOUT INSECTS
ALL ABOUT GRASSHOPPERS

by Karen Latchana Kenney

po**g**o

Ideas for Parents and Teachers

Pogo Books let children practice reading informational text while introducing them to nonfiction features such as headings, labels, sidebars, maps, and diagrams, as well as a table of contents, glossary, and index.

Carefully leveled text with a strong photo match offers early fluent readers the support they need to succeed.

Before Reading

- "Walk" through the book and point out the various nonfiction features. Ask the student what purpose each feature serves.
- Look at the glossary together. Read and discuss the words.

Read the Book

- Have the child read the book independently.
- Invite him or her to list questions that arise from reading.

After Reading

- Discuss the child's questions. Talk about how he or she might find answers to those questions.
- Prompt the child to think more. Ask: Some grasshoppers are bright colors. In the animal kingdom, this usually means the animal is poisonous. Can you name any other bright, poisonous animals?

Pogo Books are published by Jump!
5357 Penn Avenue South
Minneapolis, MN 55419
www.jumplibrary.com

Library of Congress Cataloging-in-Publication Data

Names: Kenney, Karen Latchana, author.
Title: All about grasshoppers / by Karen Latchana Kenney.
Description: Minneapolis, MN: Jump!, Inc., [2024]
Series: All about insects | Includes index.
Audience: Ages 7-10
Identifiers: LCCN 2022052147 (print)
LCCN 2022052148 (ebook)
ISBN 9798885244336 (hardcover)
ISBN 9798885244343 (paperback)
ISBN 9798885244350 (ebook)
Subjects: LCSH: Grasshoppers—Juvenile literature.
Classification: LCC QL508.A2 K358 2024 (print)
LCC QL508.A2 (ebook)
DDC 595.7/26—dc23/eng/20221031
LC record available at https://lccn.loc.gov/2022052147
LC ebook record available at https://lccn.loc.gov/2022052148

Editor: Jenna Gleisner
Designer: Emma Almgren-Bersie

Photo Credits: triocean/Shutterstock, cover; Protasov AN/Shutterstock, 1; Nature Peaceful/Shutterstock, 3; Julia Reed/iStock, 4 (top); Kriengsuk Prasroetsung/Shutterstock, 4 (bottom); zairiazmal/Shutterstock, 5; Stephen Dalton/Minden Pictures/SuperStock, 6-7; LagunaticPhoto/iStock, 8-9; Holger Kirk/Shutterstock, 10; Grafissimo/iStock, 11; Nicola Colombo/Alamy, 12-13; Sainam51/Shutterstock, 14-15; blickwinkel/Alamy, 16; Somyot Mali-ngam/Shutterstock, 17; DjMiko/iStock, 18-19 (left); Jen Watson/Shutterstock, 18-19 (right); Glass and Nature/Shutterstock, 20-21; EcoPrint/Shutterstock, 23.

Printed in the United States of America at Corporate Graphics in North Mankato, Minnesota.

TABLE OF CONTENTS

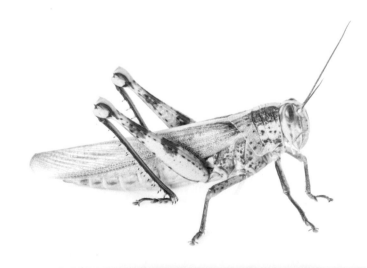

CHAPTER 1

GREETINGS, GRASSHOPPER!

A green **insect** jumps into the air! It lands in the grass.

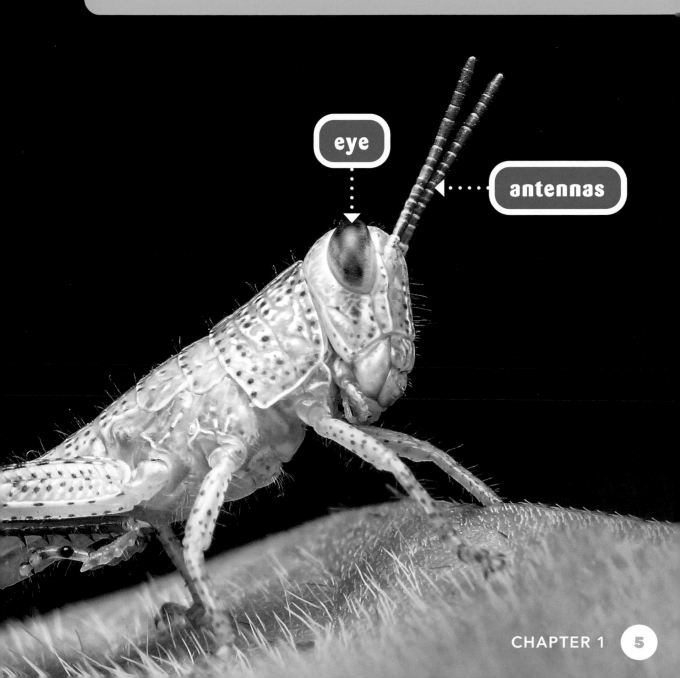

Two **antennas** move and feel. Big, round eyes look for plants to eat. Who is this hopper? It is a grasshopper!

eye

antennas

wing

A grasshopper uses its antennas to touch and smell. **Organs** on the grasshopper's abdomen or legs hear sounds. Strong back legs make it an amazing jumper. It flies with two pairs of wings.

TAKE A LOOK!

What are the parts of a grasshopper? Take a look!

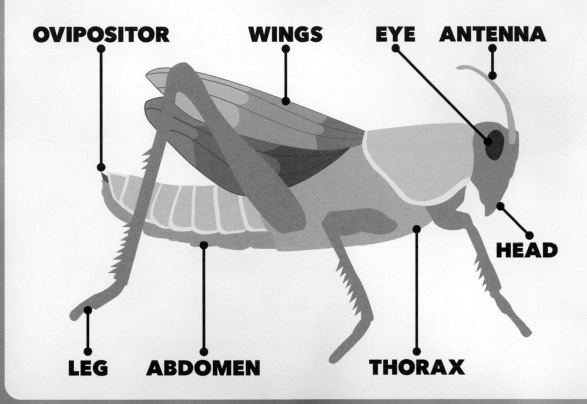

OVIPOSITOR WINGS EYE ANTENNA

HEAD

LEG ABDOMEN THORAX

More than 11,000 grasshopper **species** live around the world. Many are green or brown. They match the plants they live near.

Others are bright and colorful. The eastern lubber grasshopper is yellow. Its bright color tells **predators** that it is **poisonous**.

eastern lubber grasshopper

CHAPTER 2

GRASS DWELLERS

A large grasshopper lands on a wheat plant. It starts chewing the wheat. It eats bite after bite.

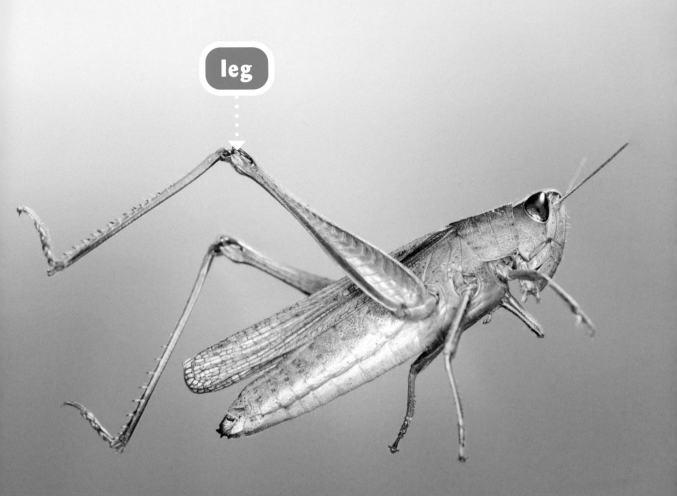

leg

Soon, it is time to find more food. The grasshopper folds its back legs. They lie flat. Then, the grasshopper quickly pops its legs up. It hops into the air!

Many grasshoppers live alone in prairies and grasslands. In these **habitats**, plants grow low to the ground. There is plenty of food for grasshoppers to eat.

DID YOU KNOW?

Not all grasshoppers live in dry grasses. Some live near water. They eat plants that grow in wet soil. Some can even dive and swim!

Camouflage helps grasshoppers hide from predators. Birds, gophers, and spiders eat adult grasshoppers. Flies, beetles, and crickets eat their eggs.

DID YOU KNOW?

Some people eat grasshoppers. Why? The insects are a good source of **protein**.

CHAPTER 3

LIFE CYCLE AND SWARMS

Most grasshoppers lay their eggs in soil. An adult female uses its **ovipositor**. She digs a hole in the soil. She lays eggs in it. Then, she makes a sticky foam. It covers the eggs and turns hard. Some females lay eggs directly on plants.

foam

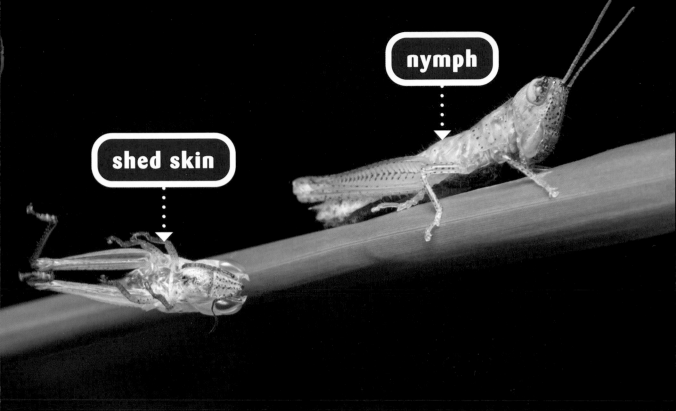

Nymphs hatch from the eggs. They look like tiny adults. As they eat plants and grow, they **molt**. They shed their skin around five times. Then, they are adults.

desert locust

swarm

Desert locusts usually live alone. But they gather in a **swarm** when food is hard to find. Joining the swarm causes their bodies to change. The locusts release a **chemical** and turn bright yellow.

The swarm **migrates** long distances. When the swarm lands, the grasshoppers eat everything they can find.

DID YOU KNOW?

Grasshoppers that swarm are called locusts. A desert locust swarm can have up to 80 million grasshoppers!

Most grasshoppers live on their own. They are friendly insects in our gardens. Look outside near your school or home. Have you seen a grasshopper?

ACTIVITIES & TOOLS

SING LIKE A GRASSHOPPER

Some grasshoppers make songs by rubbing their legs against their wings. Make your own grasshopper song with this fun activity!

What You Need:

- computer or tablet
- large craft or popsicle stick
- plastic comb
- paper
- pencil

1 Use a computer or tablet to search for and listen to grasshopper songs.

2 Rub the craft stick along the edges of the comb. Does it sound like a grasshopper?

3 Grasshoppers stop and start during their songs. Try making songs like the ones you heard with the comb and craft stick.

4 Then, make your own song. Write down how many long parts, short parts, and stops it has. Play your grasshopper song for a family member or friend.

GLOSSARY

antennas: Feelers on the head of an insect.

camouflage: A disguise or natural coloring that allows animals to hide by making them look like their surroundings.

chemical: A liquid the body produces.

habitats: The places where animals or plants are usually found.

insect: A small animal with three pairs of legs, one or two pairs of wings, and three main body parts.

migrates: Moves to another area or climate at a particular time of year.

molt: To shed an old, outer skin so that a new one can grow.

nymphs: Young grasshoppers in the larvae stage.

organs: Parts of the body that have certain purposes.

ovipositor: An organ used by an insect to dig holes and lay eggs.

poisonous: Having a substance that can harm or kill a person, animal, or plant.

predators: Animals that hunt other animals for food.

protein: A nutrient in food that helps build and heal body tissue.

species: One of the groups into which similar animals and plants are divided.

swarm: A large group of flying insects.

INDEX

TO LEARN MORE

Finding more information is as easy as 1, 2, 3.

1 **Go to www.factsurfer.com**

2 **Enter "grasshoppers" into the search box.**

3 **Choose your book to see a list of websites.**

FACT SURFER